WESS
for you and your dog

Dedicated to BOUNTY
My faithful chum and companion

Patricia M Wilnecker
1993

By the same author:

non-fiction
High Street Murders 1598
Published by Poole Museum Services
A History of Upper Parkstone (beginning to 1939)
Upper Parkstone in the Second World War
More Recollections of Old Upper Parkstone
Bounty, the tale of a dog
Published by Patricia M Wilnecker

fiction:
The Bountifull Gyfte
Published by Patricia M Wilnecker

Published by Patricia M Wilnecker
73 Gwynne Road
Parkstone
Poole, Dorset
BH12 2AR

First published 1993
© P M Wilnecker

British Library Cataloguing in Publication Data
A catalogue record for this book is available from the British Library

All rights reserved
ISBN 0 9513971 5 X

Typeset in Palatino 10/11 and printed in Great Britain by The Local History Press, 3 Devonshire Promenade, Lenton, Nottingham NG7 2DS.

CONTENTS

A map showing the locations of the walks can be found on pages 18 & 19.

WALK	LOCATION	PAGE
1	Keyhaven	6
2	Linford Bottom, New Forest	6
3	Rockford Common, New Forest	6
4	High Corner, New Forest	7
5	Abbotswell, New Forest	7
6	Castle Hill, Burley	8
7	Breamore Mizmaze	8
8	Martin Down	9
9	Gussage all Saints	9
10	Hambledon Hill	9
11	Hod Hill	10
12	Okeford Hill	10
13	Milldown, Blandford	10
14	Spetisbury Rings	11
15	Badbury Rings	11
16	Kingston Lacy boundary	11
17	Pamphill Green	12
18	Stanpit Marshes, Purewell	12
19	Hengistbury Head	13
20	Iford Bridge to Tuckton Bridge	13
21	Tuckton/Wick/Hengistbury Head/Tuckton	13
22	St Catherines Hill, Christchurch	14
23	Muscliffe River Walk	14
24	Throop Mill Circular	15
25	Strouden	15
26	Talbot Woods/Slade Farm	15
27	Pugs Hole	16
28	Meyrick Park	16
29	Redhill Common	17
30	Bournemouth Gardens	17
31	West Cliff, Bournemouth	17
32	Branksome Chine Woods	20

continued overleaf....

33	Branksome Cliffs	20
34	Canford Cliffs Chine	20
35	Overlinks Gardens, Parkstone	21
36	Blake Hill, Parkstone	21
37	Sandbanks Beach/Midway Path	22
38	Luscombe Valley	22
39	Talbot Heath	23
40	Herbert Avenue Recreation Ground	23
41	Alexandra Park, Parkstone	23
42	Baiter/Poole Park Bunny	24
43	Rockley/Ham Common	24
44	Holmwood, Longham	24
45	Matcham's View Railway Walk	25
46	Avon Forest South	25
47	Avon Forest North	25
48	Canford Heath	26
49	Broadstone Recreation Ground	26
50	Delph Woods	27
51	Wareham Forest	27
52	Wareham/Redcliff/Wareham	28
53	Bloxworth/Woodbury Hill/Bloxworth	28
54	South Haven Point/Bramble Bay/Jerrys Point	29
55	Shell Bay to Studland	29
56	Studland to Old Harry Rocks	30
57	Agglestone, Studland Heath	30
58	Durleston Country Park	31
59	Corfe Castle Common	31
60	Kimmeridge	32
61	Grange Arch, Purbeck	32
62	Encombe Hill, Purbeck	33
63	Swyre Head, Purbeck	33
64	Hill Bottom, Purbeck	33
65	Thorncombe/Black Heath	34
66	Sutton Poyntz	34
67	Ringstead	35
68	Maumbury Rings	35
69	Maiden Castle	36
70	Hardy's Monument	36

PREFACE

You will find that these walks are 'suggested locations' rather than detailed instructions, so it might be as well to take the relevant Ordnance Survey map with you for longer ones in the country.

There are several excellent books listing detailed walks around and about this area but personally I find when I am walking with my dog that I am keeping one eye on him and the other on the scenery. These detailed walks often need rapt attention or one can get hopelessly lost. This book, then, is for people who like to explore freely without too much concentration and the walks are entirely or mainly 'off the lead' for your dog.

Time and again I have met dog owners who say, 'It's a job to find somewhere different to take them', so I started by listing all the walks Bounty and I have done, and this book was the result. You will find short walks, too. These may or may not be new to you, but those in the towns are useful if you are shopping or sightseeing and would like your dog to have an 'off the lead' run as compensation.

Do remember though, when in the countryside dogs must be under control in the vicinity of livestock and that farmers are perfectly within their rights to shoot those which worry their animals - and I would hate to have that on my conscience.

With this warning in mind, I wish you and your dog many happy hours together enjoying our beautiful Wessex.

NB. Where pubs and eating places are listed they are not necessarily starting points for the walks, but are conveniently near by car and will all accommodate dogs in one way or another.

Beaches, Southbourne to Sandbanks

Most of these are closed to dogs from 1st May to 30th September inclusive but they ARE allowed on the promenade on a lead. There are limited areas where they CAN go on the beach, however. Check the notice boards on the seafront for current information. For the rest of the year the beaches are unrestricted - but PLEASE DO CLEAN UP AFTER YOUR DOG, whether the signs say so or not - it is only fair to other beach users, and gives all dog owners a bad reputation if you do not.

These walks were all correct at the time of going to press, but places are liable to change. If you come across any of these or have any other favourite walks in Wessex suitable for dogs, or indeed comments on any of my books, please let me know. My address is on page 2.

WALK 1   KEYHAVEN
DURATION: *approximately 1½ hrs.*
STARTING POINT: *Keyhaven Harbour, near Milford on Sea.*
FOOD: *The Gun Inn, Keyhaven. Dogs welcome on a lead.*

Park in the Pay and Display car park opposite the Gun Inn (free in winter) if there is no room alongside the harbour. Head east over the bridge then follow the shoreline along a raised dyke. The walk skirts a nature reserve but this is safely fenced with sheep wire. There are fine views across to Hurst Castle, the Needles and the northern coast of the Isle of Wight. The shoreline is muddy at low tide with wading birds in profusion at different times of the year. The masts of Lymington boatyards can be seen ahead, but to make this a circular walk, on reaching a gate across the path go through it and turn inland, crossing over a footbridge. Still bearing left, take a wide track which leads you back to Keyhaven.

WALK 2   LINFORD BOTTOM, NEW FOREST
DURATION: *flexible.*
STARTING POINT: *Linford Car Park, near Ringwood.*
FOOD: *High Corner Inn. Dogs welcome. (See High Corner Walk for directions.)*

From Ringwood take the road to Hangersley, then follow the signpost to Linford. On the edge of the New Forest, this walk takes you from any of the three car parks (one with toilets) into unsurpassed heath and woodland with the added bonus of clear, gravelly streams for your dog to splash around in. If you are feeling adventurous you could follow the main brook past Great Linford Inclosure and Red Shoot Wood to High Corner Wood and the High Corner Inn, but rather than give detailed directions I suggest you consult and take with you a large scale Ordnance Survey map. A lovely walk.

WALK 3   ROCKFORD COMMON
DURATION: *flexible.*
STARTING POINT: *Moyles Court, near Ringwood.*
FOOD: *Red Shoot Inn, on Moyles Court to Linwood Road. Dogs welcome.*

Not far from Ringwood on the right of the A338 road to Salisbury, take the lane that leads to Moyles Court. Near the ford by the school and cross roads, a 'no through road' leads uphill to a sandpit where there is plenty of room to park. Walk on up the hill either by the surfaced lane through a gate barrier or up the steeper track to a solitary tree. A circular walk can be taken around the perimeter of a disused gravel pit, now almost unrecognisable with its disguise of brambles and gorse. This takes ¾hr, or continue on and explore the open common if you want a longer walk. Very pleasant country, and safe 'off the lead'.

WALK 4   HIGH CORNER, NEW FOREST
DURATION: *flexible.*
STARTING POINT: *High Corner, off Moyles Court - Linwood Road.*
FOOD: *High Corner Inn. Dogs welcome.*

From the A338 Ringwood to Salisbury Road take the unclassified lane to Moyles Court and thence the Linwood road, until you reach a rough track on the left (about 3 miles from the A338). High Corner Inn is signposted and there is a large car park. There are excellent walks through heath and woodland all around you to explore at will, with a good hostelry nearby. The views stretch to wide horizons and this is fine walking at any time of the year.

WALK 5   ABBOTSWELL, NEW FOREST
DURATION: *flexible.*
STARTING POINT: *Abbotswell, near Frogham.*
FOOD: *Convenient pub: The Foresters Arms, Abbotswell Road. Well-behaved dogs welcome on a lead.*

This is as glorious a stretch of unspoilt open forest as you could wish for, just as enjoyable on a frosty day in winter as in the heat of summer.

From the A338 Ringwood-Salisbury road, go off the bypass into Fordingbridge and turn right, taking the Stuckton/Frogham road which leads directly to Abbotswell. The large, free car park for this walk is approximately 500 yards past the Foresters Arms, on top of the hill to the right. Eastwards in the distance is Amberwood Enclosure. North east is Hampton Ridge and south east of Latchmoor Brook which runs along the valley is Sloden Enclosure where there was a pottery in Roman times. I usually take the gravel track downhill to the brook, but there are so many lovely walks to choose from that I will leave you to explore for yourself.

WALK 6   CASTLE HILL, BURLEY

DURATION: *approx 1 hour excluding exploration of the village.*
STARTING POINT: *Castle Hill car park, Picket Post to Burley Road from Ringwood.*
FOOD: *Coach House Tearooms (summer only). Nowhere accepts dogs in winter.*

From the Picket Post to Burley road turn sharp right after about 1 mile to Castle Hill car park. Climb the rough path up the hill and follow the gravel lane. There are good views from the top when you pause to get your breath! The 'castle' is an ancient earthwork and its rings are visible here. Just past Blackbush Cottages on the left a stile leads you through woodland, over a couple of rustic bridges and runs alongside the drive of a grandiose modern house. By the wrought iron gate it is 'on the lead' I'm afraid. Turn right at the road and after a few yards, cross over to a safe, raised footpath that takes you into Burley village. Donkeys and ponies often stand around, surveying the cars with disinterest. Go through the village, turn right and continue for about a quarter of a mile until you reach Castle Hill Lane (off the lead again) which will take you back to your starting place.

WALK 7   BREAMORE MIZ-MAZE

DURATION: *approx $2^1/_2$ miles return.*
STARTING POINT: *Breamore House car park.*
FOOD: *The Rose and Thistle, Rockbourne. Although a sign reads 'no dogs', the Landlord assured me that well-behaved dogs are allowed.*

Breamore is reached from the A338 Ringwood to Salisbury road, 3 miles north of Fordingbridge. From the rear of Breamore House, which dates from 1572, a footpath leads uphill through the woods, then emerges into open countryside. There are fine views on this walk and no danger from traffic as you are far from 'civilisation'. The Miz-Maze, which is in trees at the top of the next hill, was cut into the turf in ancient times and adapted by the monks in the Middle Ages for the special rites of the church. It is only about 90 ft in diameter but the pattern is so intricate that it is said to 'walk it' would take up to 15 minutes. That is not possible nowadays however, as there is a fence protecting it from the ravages of time and feet. Also of interest on your return is Breamore church which is Saxon in origin and was built around 980AD.

WALK 8   MARTIN DOWN
DURATION: *flexible.*
STARTING POINT: *Martin Village.*
FOOD: *The Coote Arms on the A354 Blandford-Salisbury Road. Dogs welcome.*

Martin village is on the borders of Hampshire and Wiltshire. The Down is a wide expanse of open grassland rising to 528 feet above sea level, rolling down from Ackling Dyke, an ancient trackway which marks the county boundary and is a site of special scientific interest. From the village, look for a green triangle of grass near a telephone kiosk. From there, go along Sillens Lane which is a long, narrow road and leads directly to a free car park. One of the last areas of ancient downland, this is a fine place for wild flowers and butterflies in summer with wide, expansive views over the surrounding countryside.

WALK 9   GUSSAGE ALL SAINTS
DURATION: *flexible.*
STARTING POINT: *Drovers Inn, Gussage All Saints.*
FOOD: *Drovers Inn. Dogs welcome.*

From the B3078 Wimborne to Cranborne road turn left at the Horton Inn (a large white building on your left), then follow the signpost to Gussage All Saints. There is a large car park behind the Drovers which you may use IF you are visiting it later, which I can recommend. Take the footpath alongside the Inn and turn left at the 'T' junction where it joins another wide track. Continue on and explore the footpaths at will. At the bottom of the valley the way runs alongside woodland. Safe for dogs, as the paths by fields are mostly 'sheep fenced' with squared wire mesh - but there are plenty of rabbity scents, so my dog assures me!

WALK 10   HAMBLEDON HILL
DURATION: *flexible.*
STARTING POINT: *Outskirts of Child Okeford.*
FOOD: *Royal Oak, Okeford Fitzpaine. Dogs welcome, but closed Wednesday lunchtimes.*

Park in the layby about 150 yards past two groups of cottages on the road southeast out of Child Okeford. By the side of the first house, a waymarked footpath leads up to Hambledon Hill (603 ft). This fine hill fort has been here since Neolithic times and affords excellent views of the surrounding countryside. Quite steep in places, so not for the faint hearted!

WALK 11   HOD HILL
DURATION: *flexible.*
STARTING POINT: *Half mile along the Child Okeford road from A350.*
FOOD: *Royal Oak, Okeford Fitzpaine. Dogs welcome but closed Wednesday afternoons.*

From the A350 Blandford to Shaftesbury road take the turning left to Child Okeford. About half a mile on the left is a parking place on a bend with waymarked signs to Hod Hill. At about 469 ft above sea level, it is smaller but no less imposing than its neighbouring Hambledon Hill. You will find a footpath leading up to a Roman Fort. There is wild flower reserve, managed by the Dorset Trust for Nature Conservation and in late spring/early summer it abounds with blossom and butterflies. A lovely walk.

WALK 12   OKEFORD HILL, TURNWORTH
DURATION: *flexible.*
STARTING POINT: *Car park, Okeford Hill.*
FOOD: *Royal Oak, Okeford Fitzpaine. Dogs welcome but closed Wednesdays.*

It is worth going to the top of Okeford Hill (554 ft) for the superb panorama across Blackmore Vale and into Somerset to the west. Leave your car in the car park at the west side of the road then cross over where a track leads to Okeford Hill, and the misleadingly named Wareham Forest (which is nowhere near Wareham!). Tracks from here lead through woodland and out into open country with many paths asking to be explored. A fine, safe walk for your dog.

WALK 13   MILLDOWN
DURATION: *flexible.*
STARTING POINT: *A350 north from Blandford.*
FOOD: *White Horse Inn, Shaston Road, Stourpaine. Dogs allowed in public bar.*

On the outskirts of the town you will see a Milldown Middle School sign on the left. Opposite this there is a free car park alongside Milldown First School. In front of you is a large, open grassy area surrounded by a tarmac path for approximately one mile, handy in wet weather, where dogs may run free in safety, while to the north the park extends into adjacent downland. There are fine views of the massive Bryanston Public School, rebuilt at the turn of the century from bricks made at Parkstone.

WALK 14   SPETISBURY RINGS
DURATION: *about an hour*
STARTING POINT: *Spetisbury Village.*

Spetisbury Rings, also known as Crawford Castle, is an ancient Iron Age hill fort on the A350 Poole to Blandford road. Park in Spetisbury village. Leaving the garage/petrol station on your left, take the next turning left following the sign, 'Bridle path, South Farm' under a railway bridge. A footpath about 150 yards along the road on the left leads to Spetisbury Rings where you will discover fine views over the Stour Valley and surrounding countryside. Part of the Rings was destroyed by the construction of the now defunct railway line in 1857 when at least 80 skeletons were found. The platform and line of the track is still discernable.

WALK 15   BADBURY RINGS
DURATION: *flexible.*
STARTING POINT: *Badbury Rings car park.*
FOOD: *Pamphill Tearooms. Dogs allowed outside only.*

Reached from the B3082 Wimborne-Blandford road and, as this is an ancient monument, clearly signposted. The Rings, an Iron Age hill fort, are at a confluence of several Roman roads and were the scene of a major battle between the Durotriges tribe and Emperor Vespasian's Second Legion in AD 44-45. The area is now owned by the National Trust and dogs are no longer allowed into the Rings at any time as sheep graze there to conserve the natural flora. However, parking is free and there is still plenty of space for your dog to run off the lead. A clearly waymarked track leads past the Rings to the north-east. By following it and bearing right you can make this into a circular walk, emerging from Heron Drive into the beech lined main road and back to the car park.

WALK 16   KINGSTON LACY BOUNDARY
DURATION: *approximately 1 hour.*
STARTING POINT: *Opposite Lodge Farm on the B3082*
FOOD: *Pamphill Tearooms. Dogs outside only.*

At the beginning of the avenue of beech trees on the B3082 Wimborne-Blandford road and opposite Lodge Farm (a medieval hunting lodge) there is a small car park on your left. An often muddy track, Kingston Lacy Drove, leads through a gateway and alongside the parkland of Kingston Lacy house where many mature trees were felled by the great storm of October 1987. A circular walk can be taken by bearing first right along the prettily named Sweetbriar Drove at the bridle path signpost. Walk as far again, then take the next bridle path to the right. This is a wide, safe, grassy area and leads back to the main road where the broad verge makes comfortable walking back to the car park. (Beware of the busy road though). This walk is on National Trust property and passes through fields with good views of Badbury Rings.

WALK 17   PAMPHILL GREEN
DURATION: *short walk, but flexible.*
STARTING POINT: *Wimborne-Blandford road, Pamphill.*
FOOD: *Vine Inn, Pamphill. Dogs welcome.*

From the B3082 Wimborne to Blandford road take the turning for Pamphill. Go past the Pamphill Farm Shop and Dorset County Saddlery and, by the church, turn left where an avenue of oak trees planted in 1846 imitates the larger, two mile beech avenue alongside Badbury Rings, planted eleven years earlier. The area is owned by the National Trust but dogs can run free on the wide green.

The walk may be extended by exploring the marked footpaths which lead off the green and, if you have time, this is worth doing, as you will discover truly rural Dorset with the old cottages and Pamphill Manor standing back from the open grassy area. The small thatched pavilion is the home of the Kingston Lacy Cricket Club which was established in 1904.

WALK 18   STANPIT MARSHES PUREWELL
DURATION: *flexible.*
STARTING POINT: *Stanpit.*
FOOD: *The Ship in Distress Spud Pub, Stanpit. Dogs allowed in public lounge bar.*

From Purewell, take the Stanpit road. Almost opposite Bub Lane there is a free gravelled car park by a recreation ground. This can be a very pleasant circular walk alongside the recreation ground to the River Stour. You continue along its bank towards Christchurch and return by the side of a golf course. There are fine views across the wide, shallow harbour to Hengistbury Head. Ponies and cattle graze on the marshes and many species of waterfowl can be observed. A small hut belonging to the Reserve usually displays on a notice board the varieties that may be seen that day, so bring your binoculars!

WALK 19   HENGISTBURY HEAD
DURATION: *flexible.*
STARTING POINT: *Broadway car park.*
FOOD: *Mudeford Beach cafe. Dogs outside only.*

This is an ancient monument and site of special scientific interest. There is a Pay and Display car park at the far end of the Broadway. Leaflets describing waymarked trails and giving information can be obtained from the Rangers Information Office nearby or just explore at will, but you are requested to keep to the marked paths to prevent erosion. I avoid the 'main' road as this is used by the Land Train, cyclists and delivery vehicles for the shop and cafe at Mudeford Sandspit. (There is a speed limit of 10 mph though.) By following the paths you could find the lily ponds, unexpectedly half-way down the Head on the north side, also a large lake a little further on which was formed by the old iron ore workings and now a wild life sanctuary.

There used to be a fine view of Christchurch Priory from the Head but in recent years it has been ruined by the building of modern riverside houses - all right in their place, but this is certainly NOT it. The Hampshire Avon and Dorset Stour converge near Christchurch and flow into the sea through the harbour. By the black house at the end of the sandy peninsula and its beach huts is the Avon Run. The currents are very strong here and swans may be seen racing through at a rate of knots!

WALK 20   IFORD BRIDGE TO TUCKTON BRIDGE
DURATION: *about half an hour.*
STARTING POINT: *Old Bridge Road, Iford.*

Park near the old bridge where ducks dabble and splash. There has been a bridge here since 1140. The present old bridge was built in 1784 and carried the main road traffic to Christchurch before vehicles became too heavy for it and it was replaced in 1933 by the modern one. The path follows the river along a pleasant walk to Tuckton.

WALK 21   TUCKTON/WICK MEADOWS/HENGISTBURY HEAD/RETURN BY FERRYBOAT
DURATION: *all day.*
STARTING POINT: *Wick Lane, Tuckton.*
FOOD: *Mudeford Beach Cafe. Dogs outside only.*

This makes a good day's outing if your dog doesn't mind boats! Park in the free car park at Wick Lane, Tuckton (near Tuckton Bridge) and follow the footpath alongside the river Stour. This eventually brings you via Wick Meadows to Hengistbury Head and Mudeford Beach with its residential beach huts (which may be rented). Dogs are allowed on the beach but a friendly sign asks you to keep them under control. Ferry boats run frequently from the Mudeford jetty (Weather and time of year permitting. Check with Mudeford Beach Superintendent telephone 0202 423473.) and will take you back to Tuckton.

WALK 22   ST CATHERINE'S HILL, CHRISTCHURCH
DURATION: *flexible.*
STARTING POINT: *Marlow Drive, St Catherine's Hill.*
FOOD: *The Catherine Wheel. Dogs allowed in public bar.*

From the Bournemouth to Ringwood spur road take the turning at Blackwater Bridge for Christchurch. At the first roundabout turn left where there is a signpost to St Catherine's Hill by a parade of shops (Marlow Drive). At the junction with Hillside Drive is a five-bar gate with a sign, 'Woodland Walk'. This leads uphill to a wide expanse of pinewoods and heatherland. There is a choice of many paths but I would recommend heading east to the rim of the old gravel pit where there are expansive views across the Avon valley to the New Forest. A straight track below you follows the line of the old Christchurch to Ringwood railway. Seats on a headland to the south east are well placed to contemplate the view. Dudsmoor Farm is before you, with Hengistbury Head and Christchurch Priory to the far right. If you follow the waymarked posts, number 10 is by another seat with views over Bournemouth with the Gothic-looking watertower of Southbourne on the skyline. The nearby mysterious space-age dome is a covered reservoir.

WALK 23   MUSCLIFFE RIVER WALK
DURATION: *flexible.*
STARTING POINT: *Granby Road car park.*
FOOD: *Cooper Dean Arms, Castle Lane West. Dogs outside only.*

This walk is on the very edge of Bournemouth and looks out across open countryside. From Castle Lane, Muscliffe Lane is the road to follow. Just past a fine old white farm house with holm oaks overhanging the road on your left is Granby Road. Immediately on your right is Stourvale Recreation Ground and a free, gravelled car park. You may walk along the river bank to the left or right. The paths are clearly marked and your dog is safe off the lead. (But beware of anglers' fish hooks!) Signs point to Berry Hill and Throop Village via Wilderness Way to the east, with Redhill and Water Lane Farm via Meadows Walk to the west. A very pleasant area.

WALK 24   THROOP MILL, CIRCULAR WALK
DURATION: *approximately 1½hrs .*
STARTING POINT: *Throop Mill, Throop Road.*
FOOD: *Cooper Dean Arms, Castle Lane West. Dogs outside only.*

Park at the free car park near the mill and cross the bridge, following the waymarked footpath along the river bank. There is some 'road work' on this walk - along Hurn Court Road and Merritown Lane - but both are 'no through roads' so quite quiet and you pass some old farmhouses (Hurn Court Farm and Dales House) which are of interest. At one point, although it cannot be seen you are quite near Hurn Airport. The walk returns along a footpath and across fields to the river - pleasant as an evening walk in summer.

WALK 25   STROUDEN
DURATION: *short walk.*
STARTING POINT: *Opposite the Hampshire Centre, Castle Lane, Bournemouth.*

Drive into Bradpole Road where you will find a recreation field and children's play area with a path leading from it to higher, wooded ground. Follow a 'natural' path through the woodland and skirt the playing fields of Summerbee School. The path broadens out into more pinewoods, and at the top of the hill is another public playing field adjoining the North Cemetery.

WALK 26   TALBOT WOODS/SLADE FARM
DURATION: *short, but extendible.*
STARTING POINT: *Alton Road, Wallisdown.*

From the right-angled bend in Alton Road a gravelled track behind St Mark's churchyard leads past fields to the pinewoods - a piece of rural Wallisdown left behind by time. Beyond the woods was Talbot (later Slades) Farm until about 20 years ago when the fields where livestock grazed were made into recreation grounds. There are several entrances to this area and many paths to explore.

Talbot Model Village was built in the 1860's by the Misses Talbot. There were originally 19 cottages, each standing in its own acre of land facing Wallisdown Road. Through the trees are the old Almshouses and St Mark's School, while Slades Lane - a rough track - leads from Wallisdown Road to Slades Farm Road. A favourite exercise area for dogs.

WALK 27   PUGS HOLE, BRANKSOME
DURATION: *about 20 mins.*
STARTING POINT: *Glenferness Avenue.*
Easily passed by unseen, this pine-clad ravine was part of the old route taken by smugglers on their way from the coast to Kinson and it is not difficult to imagine the scene on a murky winter's afternoon. Reached from Glenferness Avenue almost opposite the turning for Walford Road, the path leads into the woods alongside a small, rectangular brick building. The more adventurous (and nimble!) can follow the blue waymarker posts which lead up and along the steep sides of the ravine, whilst the more staid may amble leisurely along the valley bottom, where there are several seats to rest and watch the wild life. The large buildings behind the railings to the west belong to the private Talbot Heath School.

WALK 28   MEYRICK PARK, BOURNEMOUTH
DURATION: *approximately 1¼hrs.*
STARTING POINT: *From Central Drive, by Bournemouth Town Hall.*
To the north of Central Drive a rather pot-holed but free car park can be found between the trees about 200 yards before the railway bridge. From there, an undulating path is liberally marked by yellow paint on trees - mainly Scots pine, chestnut and oak - which takes you right around the perimeter of the 60 acre golf course, reputedly the first municipal one in the country. Keep to the marked paths and off the greens and fairways as golf balls could prove a danger! There are some good and unusual views of Bournemouth on this walk.

There is another walk on the opposite side of Central Drive which is sheltered by pine trees in hot or rainy weather and you can also keep to tarmac surfaced paths if it is wet.

Before it became a 154 acre park, this whole area was known as 'Poors Common' and was previously land reserved in trust by Sir George Meyrick as a park in compensation for loss of commoners' rights to cut turf for fuel. You may notice markers like small grave stones from time to time which bear the letter 'M' for Meyrick. These are boundary stones.

WALK 29   REDHILL COMMON
DURATION: *short walk.*
STARTING POINT: *Redhill Avenue, Moordown, Bournemouth.*
The common is bisected by Redhill Avenue. To the right going downhill there is a real 'doggy paradise' where regulars meet and dogs can play safely together on grassy areas away from the road. But beware if they enter the bushes after squirrels as dogs have come to grief here from speeding cars in Redhill Avenue. On the opposite side of the road there are football pitches and beyond them pine trees - a favourite walk in wet weather as the trees give some shelter.

WALK 30   BOURNEMOUTH GARDENS
DISTANCE: *approximately 2 miles each way.*
STARTING POINT: *Surrey Road (western end) or Coy Pond Road.*
FOOD: *Bournemouth Corporation cafe at the Tennis Centre. Dogs outside only.*
In Surrey Road near the railway viaducts there is an entrance to the gardens down some steps by a pillar box. Alternatively you may park in Coy Pond Road on the opposite side of the gardens. At Coy Pond, ducks and swans swim in a beautiful setting beneath the willows, a site often chosen by photographers for wedding photographs. The walk takes you right into Bournemouth Central Gardens through both natural and cultivated areas. There are many fine trees, with some species labelled for your information. The Bourne stream which gives Bournemouth its name runs through the gardens and is usually very clear if your dog wants a swim. Take care, though, as the gardens are intersected by roads. When you reach the flyover bridge, signs tell you your dog must be on a lead but until then they can run free. When you reach the large white War Memorial with its guardian stone lions you have reached the centre of Bournemouth.

WALK 31   WEST CLIFF, BOURNEMOUTH
DURATION: *short walk.*
STARTING POINT: *West Hill Road.*
I prefer this walk on a wild winter's day when the clifftop is deserted and there is plenty of space to park in West Hill Road, but nevertheless it is pleasant at any time of the year. There are grassy stretches interspersed with pines and footpaths where squirrels and pigeons scamper and strut. The paths lead westward to Durley Chine and the beach, so you could

18

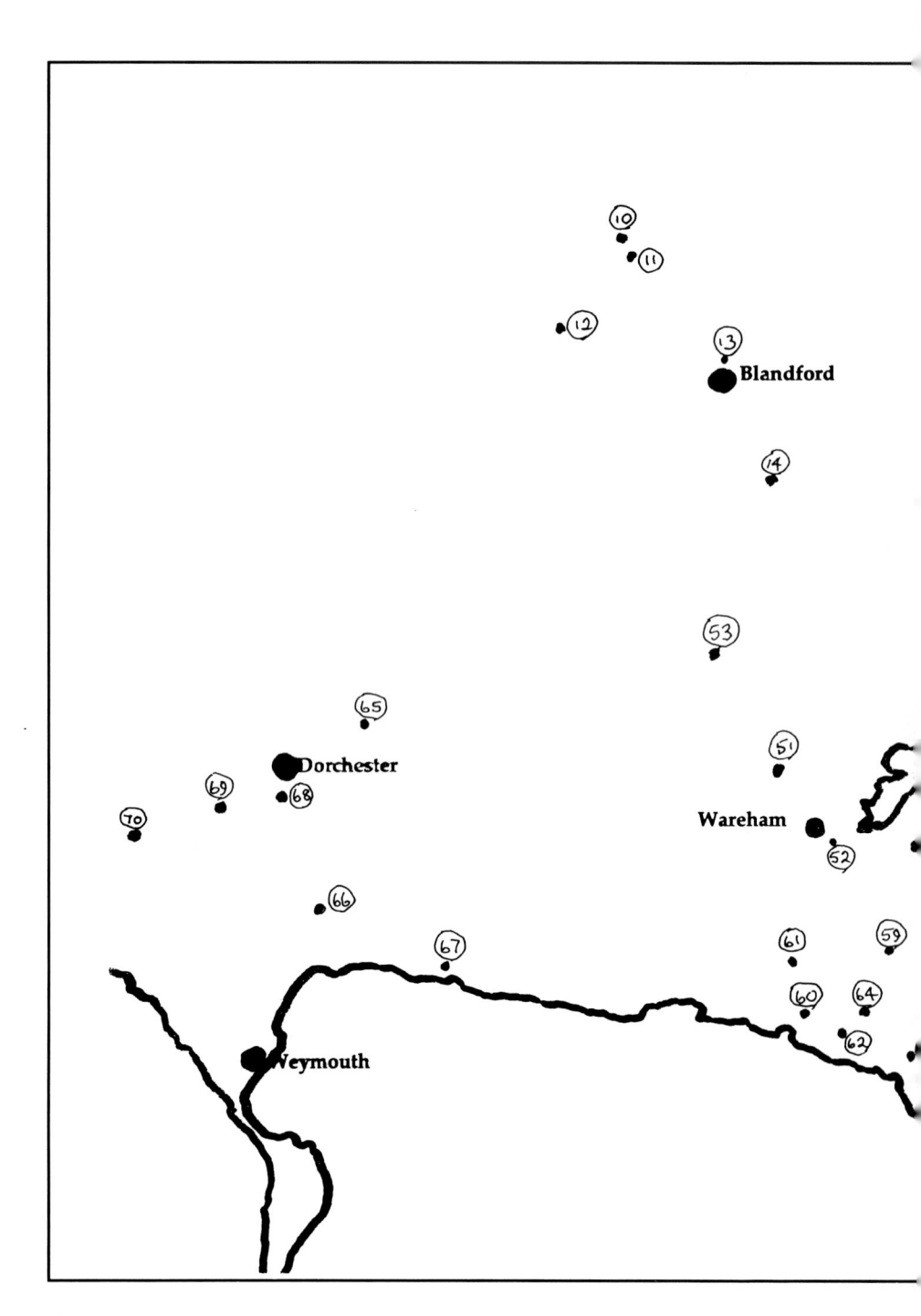

19

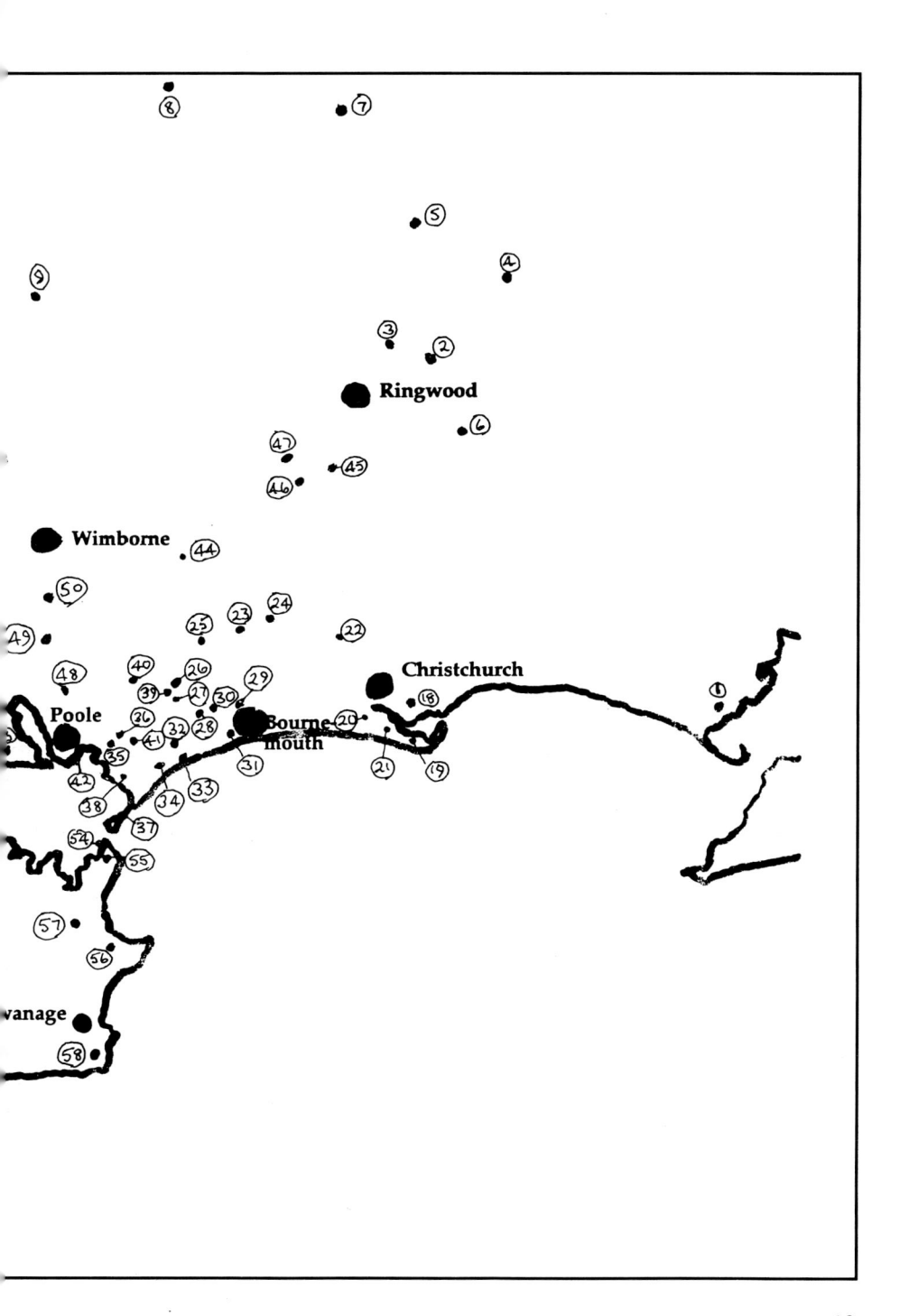

extend your walk in this direction. (Beach closed to dogs 1st May - 30th September. Allowed on the Promenade on a lead.)

WALK 32   BRANKSOME CHINE WOODS
DISTANCE: *approximately 4 miles return.*
STARTING POINT: *St Aldhelm's Close, Branksome.*
FOOD: *Beach Cafe at Branksome Chine, dogs outside only. Closed at times in winter.*
Leicester Road follows the edge of the woods and a good starting place is in the free car park in St Aldhelm's Close. Nearby is a stone arch which once stood at County Gates, prior to the boundary changes in the 1970's. Mainly of Scots pine, the woods (which are cut across by roads, so take care) are 'natural' until you reach the final one next to All Saints Church. In autumn the trees here are a riot of colour with acer, chestnut, azalea, oak, birch, sycamore and other, rarer species. Squirrels abound in the trees and foxes haunt the woods by night. This is a lovely walk on a long summers evening.

WALK 33   BRANKSOME CLIFFS
DURATION: *short walk.*
STARTING POINT: *Branksome Chine car park. (Chargeable in the season.)*
At the western end of the car park a winding footpath leads uphill to Canford Cliffs, passing through a narrow wooded area inland or with superb sea views from the cliff tops across Poole Bay to Sandbanks, Purbeck and the Isle of Wight. There are formal gardens here too, with seats in sheltered spots and two steep paths leading down to the beach to make this a circular walk - but from 1st May to 30 September inclusive dogs must be on a lead on the promenade, and not allowed on the beach until you reach the far side of Branksome Chine, where there is a dog-permitted area all year round.

WALK 34   CANFORD CLIFFS CHINE
DURATION: *a short walk but leading to the beach so extendible.*
STARTING POINT: *Cliff Drive or The Esplanade, Canford Cliffs.*
A steep path leads down through chestnut and pines to the sea. A grassy area on the top is the home of squirrels and where I have also seen a fox. On the way down you will see a less steep path leading back to the right,

which makes the return journey easier especially if you have extended the walk by going along the beach. Unfortunately this beach is closed to dogs between 1st May and 30th September but they are allowed on the promenade - on a lead.

WALK 35   OVERLINKS GARDENS, PARKSTONE
DURATION: *short walk.*
STARTING POINT: *Links Avenue.*

From Canford Cliffs Road heading south, turn right at Links Road and then left into Links View Avenue. At the end of this cul-de-sac is another little-known viewpoint amidst pine trees. A pleasant, gentle stroll on a summer's evening, with two wooden seats for you to sit and admire the view, which, as the name implies, overlooks Parkstone Golf Course.

As this is only a very short walk, you may like to lengthen it by returning to Links Road, turn left to the bottom of the hill until you reach a new brown fence on the right. A signpost points to Clifton Road and you have a steep climb through pine trees up 114 shallow steps to the summit, where several little paths wind invitingly through the rhododendrons. This is Stromboli Hill, from an old field name, but how an area of Parkstone came to be named after an Italian volcano I have been unable to discover! On this viewpoint are two marble seats inscribed with the initials 'TJ'. There is also a commemorative plaque which states the area was dedicated to Thomas Jennings by his wife 'for the use and enjoyment of the inhabitants of Poole'.

WALK 36   BLAKE HILL, PARKSTONE
DURATION: *short walk.*
STARTING POINT: *Blake Hill Crescent.*

At the top of the hill in Blake Hill Crescent a public footpath leads to a little-known viewpoint. There are panoramic views across Lilliput's marina and the islands in Poole Harbour. It is mainly pinewood with some oak, chestnut and holly and in 1992 the Corporation opened up some of the views and improved the footpaths.

WALK 37   SANDBANKS BEACH, MIDWAY PATH
DURATION: *short walk in summer. Can be extended in winter.*
STARTING POINT: *Panorama Road, Sandbanks.*

One of the few beaches in the area to be open to dogs all year round. Midway Path leads down to the sea from Sandbanks Road a few hundred yards before the ferry, just after the start of the double yellow lines. In summer, dogs are allowed on the beach as far as a large sign 'No dogs beyond this point' near Sandbanks Pavilion, but from 1st October to 30th April a long walk can be taken to Bournemouth and beyond as far as Hengistbury Head.

WALK 38   LUSCOMBE VALLEY NATURE RESERVE
DURATION: *approximately 20 minutes per circuit (we usually do 2 or 3!).*
STARTING POINT: *Near the foot of Evening Hill, Poole Harbour.*

An idyllic spot in fine weather - this is a piece of unspoilt countryside surrounded by, but hidden from, civilisation and a favourite walk of my dog's. Wild roses flourish amongst the brambles, silver birches, willows and dwarf oaks. Frogs spawn here as early as January, covering the black bog to the west with writhing bodies. Green woodpeckers, blue tits, goldfinches, jenny wrens, jays, waterfowl and squirrels can be seen at different seasons and occasionally I have glimpsed a beautiful fox. Dogs love this walk with its fascinating scents but beware - it is not for the faint-hearted after rain. You will certainly need wellies as parts can be very wet and muddy.

Park in Shore Road, Brudenell Avenue or Sandbanks Road. The Reserve is entered by a stile at the western end next to a five-bar gate. This is a circular walk, crossing the steel sheet footbridge on your left about 100 yards into the reserve. The path is clear to follow and when you hear the thwack of golf balls you are skirting the beautiful Parkstone Golf Course, which can be glimpsed through the trees. Your path crosses a wooden bridge and emerges into a wide grassy stretch (where I usually see the fox) bringing you back to your starting place. It is a very safe walk for your dog, as the only road is where you came in.

Do remember, though, that this IS a nature reserve and do not let your dog disturb the wild life. Fortunately, the path goes around the perimeter and, for the most part, thick undergrowth and brambles protect the interior.

On the opposite side of Shore Road, the ornate street lamps with entwined stylised golden dolphins have been there since 1895.

WALK 39   TALBOT HEATH
DURATION: *a short walk but may be extended.*
STARTING POINT: *Merrow Avenue, off Winston Avenue via Alder Road, Parkstone.*

If you approach from this point you may park on the heath itself. Lovely and free for your dog - there are no restrictions - an obvious circular walk can be taken by setting off in either direction, crossing the stream and returning on the opposite side. The stream is the Bourne which gives Bournemouth its name where it enters the sea, but on this walk it disappears beneath a railway embankment. The heathland is how Upper Parkstone and indeed Bournemouth looked some 250 years ago. To the north east is Highmoor Farm, the last remaining farm in the area and cattle still graze in the fields, a reminder of days gone by. Kestrels quarter the heather in search of prey and I have seen a pair of rare Dartford Warblers perched on gorse at the top of the hill to the north east.

If you have more time to spare, the walk can be extended by climbing the hill to the north east and following any of the tracks. It is impossible to get lost as the lie of the land allows you to keep sight of your starting place.

WALK 40   HERBERT AVENUE RECREATION GROUND
DURATION: *1 to 2 hours.*
STARTING POINT: *Herbert Avenue, Upper Parkstone.*

I have lived in Parkstone all my life, but only recently found this one! In a dip in the road on the western side of Kemp Welch School there is a little wooded area with a path winding away through the trees. This passes a landscaped pond and opens out into several football pitches, quite hidden from the main road. At the far side a heathery slope leads to moorland and eventually to Bourne Bottom where you may wander at will. A safe, off the lead walk.

WALK 41   ALEXANDRA PARK, PARKSTONE
DURATION: *short walk.*
STARTING POINT: *Alexandra Road.*

Situated to the south of the main shopping area in Ashley Road, this walk is a favourite of the inhabitants of Parkstone. There are three entrances - two in Alexandra Road (unrestricted street parking) and the other in Palmerston Road. This is a 'natural' park with hilly, grassy areas and trees - pines and chestnut predominating. There are squirrels too, well practised in evading the dogs.

WALK 42   BAITER/POOLE PARK BUNNY
DURATION: *approximately ¾hr.*
STARTING POINT: *Baiter, Poole.*
From Poole Quay drive eastwards following the shoreline. Go past the Pay and Display car park, as a little further on is one which is free all year round. There is a grassy expanse of mainly reclaimed land where your dog can run freely and you can enjoy the superb views of Poole Harbour and Purbeck. Continue to follow the shoreline with the railway on your left. At the point where the road disappears beneath a tiny railway bridge, you follow it and emerge on the other side of the line. Follow it back along the south side of Poole Park boating lake, passing the sluice gate or 'the Bunny', a local name for a culvert or drain. The path finally emerges through a subway and you are back at your starting point.

WALK 43   ROCKLEY, HAM COMMON
DURATION: *flexible.*
STARTING POINT: *Rockley Park, Hamworthy, Poole.*
Take the road through Rockley Caravan Park. Go past the tennis court and turn left into the narrow road which runs alongside. This leads you to a free car park with unsurpassed views across Poole Harbour to Purbeck. Boats move up and down the channel to Wareham and the little dinghies from the sailing school are shepherded around by their instructors like little ducklings. Newly marked footpaths have been recently cleared, some leading to the beach (which a few feet out is rather muddy). Inland, my dog loves to swim in a beautiful clear lake which rivals the famous Blue Pool. This is heather, silver birch and gorse country and, although there are hundreds of caravans nearby, they have been carefully landscaped so as not to intrude into the scenery.

WALK 44   HOLM WOOD, LONGHAM
DURATION: *about an hour.*
STARTING POINT: *Layby on right of Poole/Ferndown road near the Angel Inn, Longham.*
FOOD: *Angel Inn, dogs outside only.*
A waymarked footpath leads from the layby into woodland which extends to Dudsbury on the southern side. There are (albeit muddy) ponds, and many footpaths to explore - also a grassy area with rabbits and bramble bushes, the latter yielding a good crop of blackberries in autumn.

WALK 45 MATCHAMS VIEW RAILWAY WALK
DURATION: *about half an hour.*
STARTING POINT: *From the Hurn Road (Matchams Lane) on the eastern side of the bridge where it crosses the A338, car park.*

A sign post points to Matchams View and the car park. The trails are waymarked by coloured posts and follow the line of the old Ringwood to Christchurch railway which ran until 1935. From the car park there are superb views, with St Catherine's Hill to the south, the Purbeck Hills to the west and the valley of the winding River Avon below you. A short walk, but safe and interesting.

WALK 46 AVON FOREST, SOUTH SIDE
DURATION: *flexible.*
STARTING POINT: *Boundary Lane car park, a few hundred yards east of the junction with Matchams Lane.*
FOOD: *Cafe at Avon Forest North. Dogs outside only.*

There is a free car park just over the rise. A footpath leads uphill from here to a wooded area, or there is a choice of going through the field where a signboard describes the history of the area. Beyond the beacon on top of the hill are gorse and heathland with extensive views over the New Forest, Isle of Wight, Purbeck, Win Green and Cranborne Chase. This is a fine walk for dogs, but like most southern heathland, beware in summer as there are adders here. A marked trailway leads from the Boundary Lane car park with informative notices indicating points of interest, or you are free to wander at will.

This walk can also be taken as an extension of the Avon Forest North Park walk.

WALK 47 AVON FOREST, NORTH PARK
DURATION: *flexible.*
STARTING POINT: *Avon Forest Park, Birch Road, St Ives, off A31 Ferndown - Ringwood road.*
FOOD: *Cafe at the Park, dogs outside only.*

This is an area of heath and woodland. You may explore at will or leaflets can be obtained from the Visitors' Centre. Part of the trail follows a track which was the ancient road from Wimborne to Ringwood. It is as narrow as a lane but was called 'The Broad way'. Gorse blooms throughout the year and the heather spreads its subtle shades of purple in August. A safe, off the lead walk.

WALK 48   CANFORD HEATH
DURATION: *flexible.*
STARTING POINT: *Layby on A349 Poole-Wimborne road, nr Poole Grammar School.*
FOOD: *Stepping Stones Inn, 180 The Broadway, Broadstone. Dogs allowed in public bar.*

There are many different starting points, as this covers such a large area, but the one referred to above is convenient coming from Bournemouth or Poole. This extensive heathland is where from ancient times the cattle from Poole were 'Driven out by the cowherds ... pasturying by the way along the Flete by the Reddsand and so to the moor under Cannford', a track which can still be recognised today. The land was part of the huge estate belonging to the Guest family (Lord Wimborne) and the wide gravelled tracks on the heath were part of the private network of roads which extended as far as Canford Cliffs, for his use and that of Lady Wimborne. Nowadays this is the haunt of sand lizard, Dartford Warbler and harmless smooth snake as well as the venomous adder. Nevertheless, a great place for dogs!

WALK 49   BROADSTONE RECREATION GROUND
DURATION: *flexible.*
STARTING POINT: *Entrance in Dunyeats Road, near the Library. Free car park.*
FOOD: *Stepping Stones Inn, 180 The Broadway, Broadstone. Dogs allowed in public bar.*

'Recreation Ground' conjures up a picture of playing fields - but this has far more to offer. There ARE two large fields which can be reached from Sharlands Close, off the Blandford Road, but these lead to an even more extensive area of natural woodland and heath - mostly pine and silver birch but with some broad-leafed trees, especially to the north of the area beyond the cricket pitch which gives the impression of semi-wild parkland. In the spring the azaleas and rhododendrons are a beautiful sight.

WALK 50   DELPH WOODS
DURATION: *flexible. 24 acres with many different walks.*
STARTING POINT: *Gravel Hill, Broadstone.*
FOOD: *Stepping Stones Inn, The Broadway, Broadstone. Dogs allowed in public bar.*

The entrance is just south of the high traffic lights at Gravel Hill on the A349 Poole-Wimborne road, left hand side facing Wimborne opposite Blackwater Drive. At the entrance a sign reads 'Broadstone Cricket Ground, Delph Woods'. Drive along the track and past the cricket pitch (beware of potholes) as there is a larger car park a little further on. Park here, then you can either follow the waymarked route for a short walk or explore at leisure. At its furthest point the Woods meet the Broadstone-Wimborne footpath/cycleway which runs along the track of the old railway line. At the end nearest your point of entry and to the left of the cricket pitch old clay workings are now flooded and one bears the name 'Deadmans's Pond'. It is not as forbidding as it sounds though, with waterlilies flowering there in the summer months. A clear stream flows through the woods - great for retrieving sticks! This is a safe, off the lead walk and very peaceful - full of birdsong and tranquillity.

WALK 51   WAREHAM FOREST
DURATION: *flexible.*
STARTING POINT: *Wareham to Bere Regis Road, Sika Trail Car Park, almost opposite The Silent Woman Pub.*
FOOD: *The Silent Woman, dogs allowed in public bar.*

An area of mostly pinewoods with some heathland and gravel tracks. There are many entrances, the main one being the Sika Trail - where a wide gravel track leads to the large, free car park. Other entrances are off the B3075 Sherford to Sandford road with laybys and car parks - but take care not to block emergency entrances for fire engines and rescue vehicles. Walks from the Sika Trail are waymarked with coloured posts, or you may roam at will through miles of trackways. Be careful if you have a small dog that likes to explore rabbit holes though, as several terriers have been lost here over the years.

WALK 52 WAREHAM/REDCLIFF/WAREHAM
DURATION: *approx 1 hour return.*
STARTING POINT: *Wareham Quay (metered car park).*
FOOD: *Antelope Inn, West Street. Well behaved dogs welcome.*

Cross the bridge and follow the river bank. This takes you past moored boats and a small marina to Redcliff which is an ancient boundary point of Poole Harbour, still recorded in the 'beating the bounds' ceremony. You may continue on past Redcliff through a boatyard but the path ends at a caravan park, so you must return the way you came. A pleasant short walk on a fine summer's evening with the peaceful sound of water lapping against the boats and with the lovely Purbeck hills to the south.

WALK 53 BLOXWORTH/WOODBURY HILL
DISTANCE: *3 miles return.*
STARTING POINT: *Bloxworth village, off the A35 Poole/Dorchester road.*
FOOD: *Convenient pub; the Cock and Bottle, Morden. Dogs very welcome.*

This walk takes you through woodland with panoramic views of the Purbeck hills as you approach Woodbury Hill. A Fair was held on this ancient hill fort from medieval times until early in the 20th century. It was a Hiring Fair where shepherds, cowherds, dairymen, carters and milkmaids could be hired, each bearing their 'badge of office'.

I have often seen deer on this walk and your dog could also enjoy the scents of rabbits, squirrels and foxes. Pheasants, too, abound in these woods, startling the walker as they explode from the undergrowth with raucous cries.

You may park near the church at Bloxworth in the 'no through road' then go through a five-bar gate to the west. A clearly defined footpath skirts the field until you reach a single gate leading into a wood (waymarked with a blue arrow). Just inside are the remains of a huge oak which, legend says, stood here since 1087. The walk then follows blue waymarkers to Woodbury Hill. When you reach a gravel road on a hilltop near a farm you have reached your destination. (A footpath and bridle path go further but they would take you to the main road.)

The return journey is along the same path you came on, but it doesn't detract from this walk which is peaceful, free and 'far from the madding crowd'.

On the way back make sure that you fork right at the green, grassy path, having descended the slope to the first gravel track - otherwise the walk is uncomplicated. The scenery is superb at any time of the year but especially in spring and autumn.

WALK 54   SOUTH HAVEN POINT/BRAMBLE BUSH BAY/JERRYS POINT + RETURN

DURATION: *approx 2 to 3 hours.*
STARTING POINT: *Sandbanks Ferry.*
FOOD: *Shell Bay Cafe near the ferry, dogs outside only.*

An area of outstanding natural beauty, this walk follows the shoreline of Poole Harbour - the largest and surely one of the most picturesque in the western world.

Leaving your car at Sandbanks, cross the harbour entrance by car ferry which runs every 15 mins or so throughout the year. The tide here ebbs and flows with spectacular speed and small craft struggle to make headway against it. When you land, follow the shore line past the cafe on your right if the tide is out. If it is in, go along the road and past the boatyard, turning right to the shore. Just around the point from the boatyard, black and white Noah's Ark-type houseboats have been moored as long as living memory. The harbour is very shallow here and at different times of the year many species of waders can be observed feeding and swimming. I have seen Dartford Warblers in the gorse and followed the tracks of deer along the shore. It can be sticky underfoot where seams of clay surface, but beware, do not be tempted to take short cuts across the mud at low tide - or you could get stuck!

A rusty hulk of a long-dead boat lies on Redhorn Quay which juts out towards the opposite peninsula of Goathorn. Oil has been discovered here but the drilling site is well concealed. Picturesque sunsets can be seen from this point on calm summer evenings, reflecting in the still waters of the harbour. A well-recommended walk.

WALK 55   SHELL BAY/STUDLAND

DISTANCE: *approximately 6 miles round trip.*
STARTING POINT: *South Haven Point.*
FOOD: *Bankes Arms, Studland. Dogs welcome.*

If travelling from Bournemouth, leave your car on the Sandbanks side of the car ferry. The walk begins on the Shell Bay side. (Lead restrictions apply May to September inclusive.) There are really wide stretches of beach, great for you and your dog but a sign around the corner cautions the unwary that there is a nudist beach here. After two more miles the path to the village will take you to the Bankes Arms for lunch. If fine, there are superb views from the pub garden and if cold, there is usually an open fire to cheer you before you retrace your steps back to the ferry.

WALK 56 STUDLAND/OLD HARRY ROCKS
DISTANCE: *approximately 1 mile.*
STARTING POINT: *Studland Village.*
FOOD: *Bankes Arms, Studland. Dogs welcome.*

Park in the car park next to the Bankes Arms (free to National Trust members) and take the footpath down Watery Lane to the beach. This was the haunt of pirates in the time of Elizabeth I and their ships had safe anchorage in Studland Bay. Walk past the beach huts on your right until you reach a footpath sign to Old Harry Rocks. Follow this for three quarters of a mile but take care as you approach the end of the bushes on the seaward side, as the cliffs are very steep here and I strongly recommend your dog to be on a lead at this point. There are fine views across Poole Bay to Bournemouth, Hengistbury Head and the Isle of Wight, with Shell Bay's beautiful stretches of sand leading the eye to Sandbanks. Shipping passes in and out of Poole Harbour's narrow entrance, with large ferries sailing to the Channel Islands and France.

WALK 57 AGGLESTONE/STUDLAND HEATH/ AGGLESTONE
DISTANCE: *3 miles return.*
STARTING POINT: *Corfe Castle/Studland Road.*
FOOD: *Convenient pub; Bankes Arms, Studland Village. Dogs welcome.*

About a quarter of a mile past the viewpoint on the road from Corfe Castle, on the left hand side as you reach the brow of a hill there is a grassy pull-in which takes about 4 cars. A sign post reads 'Footpath to Agglestone' and crosses part of the golf course before reaching the heath. The Agglestone is a huge 200 ton 16 ft high sandstone rock exposed by centuries of erosion, but legend says it was thrown from Corfe Castle by the Devil who was aiming at the Isle of Wight and missed. There are lovely views on this walk - the 5 islands in the harbour, Sandbanks, Studland Bay with Old Harry Rocks and, on a clear day, the Needles, Alum Bay and sometimes even St Catherines Point on the Isle of Wight.

A variation can be made by taking the marked path from the Agglestone to Studland village - but do not be tempted to take short cuts across the heather as it can be boggy in places.

WALK 58   DURLESTON COUNTRY PARK
DURATION: *flexible.*
STARTING POINT: *Swanage.*
FOOD: *Durleston Head Castle.*

Take the Durleston Road from Swanage and park in the large metered car park. Alternatively, walk from Anvil Point Swanage by way of the clearly marked Victorian Trail which follows the steep cliffs (so DO take care of your dog here). From the Country Park's 261 acres (opened in 1973 by Dorset County Council) there are many areas of Purbeck for you to explore. Check at the Visitors' Centre near the car park for details, or wander at will. There is a fascinating choice of woodland, farmland, downs, cliffs and sea, with all the variety of wildlife and wild flowers that these support - in early summer the cliffs are a riot of pink thrift. The waymarked theme trails all start from the Park Visitors' Centre. Nearby is the Great Globe - 40 tons of Portland stone erected in Victorian times by the famous owner of Durleston Head, stone merchant George Burt. He was also responsible for the many stone inscriptions to be found in the park.

WALK 59   CORFE CASTLE COMMON
DURATION: *flexible.*
STARTING POINT: *West Street car park, Corfe Castle.*
FOOD: *Marblers. (16th century cafe next to the PO, West Street) Through their 'out of the ordinary' gift shop is a flagstone floored small cafe. Dogs welcome. Closed Mondays all year round, and occasionally off-season.*

A stile leads from the car park across the adjacent field and alongside the hedge. (Follow the yellow waymarkers.) After about a quarter of a mile you will reach the Common. On your right you will see the ancient little stone and brick Copper Bridge. Ponies graze on the Common and in early summer in hidden corners amongst the blaze of gorse you may come across many wild orchids. The Common extends on both sides of the road to Kingston on the hill and you can explore at will. I have seen deer amongst the gorse on the eastern side.

On your return leave the Common by the gate near the horse pound which leads into West Street. There is a fine view of Corfe Castle on the way back that is missed by many visitors, and I can recommend produce and plants bought from an unattended 'trust the shopper' stall on the left. You take what you want and leave payment in an unlocked tin, helping yourself to change! Passing between cottages with evocative names you return to the car park.

An alternative start is to take the narrow passage between numbers 19-21 West Street which leads to fields. Follow the marked track across these. After crossing one road (a quiet cul-de-sac called 'The Halves') you reach the Common. This is a favourite of my dog's.

WALK 60   KIMMERIDGE
DURATION: *2 to 3 hours.*
STARTING POINT: *The disused quarry just before the road branches to Smedmore and Kimmeridge.*
FOOD: *The Seven Taps, Kimmeridge. Dogs welcome.*

Go back up the road and take the footpath above the quarry uphill along Smedmore Hill to Swyre Head, 666 feet above sea level (not to be confused with the other Dorset Swyre Head near Abbotsbury).

From there, having stopped to get your breath and admire the view of cliffs and sea, follow the waymarked footpath down the steep hill. Take care of your dog with the sheer cliffs if you use the coastal path though; you can avoid these and make the walk shorter by taking the path which passes Smedmore House. A lovely part of Dorset, with fine views to Gad Cliff and Portland.

WALK 61   GRANGE ARCH TO CORFE CASTLE
DISTANCE: *about $3^1/_2$ miles.*
STARTING POINT: *Car Park, top of hill on Stoborough/Kimmeridge road.*
FOOD: *See Corfe Castle, walk 59.*

The car park is large, free, grassy and has superb views in all directions. Creech Grange is below you to the north with the army training ranges to the west. Southwards is the fertile vale of Purbeck and beyond are the cliffs and the sea. The walk is along the ridge of the hill (652 feet above sea level) to the east near the flagpole. Follow the track via Ridgeway and Knowle Hills to Corfe Castle - but a cautionary note - there may be sheep or cattle in the adjacent fields.

WALK 62   ENCOMBE HILL, PURBECK
DURATION: *approximately 1 hour.*
STARTING POINT: *Kingston Village.*
FOOD: *Scott Arms, Kingston. Well behaved dogs and children welcome.*

Just past the largest Kingston church (the older one is disused) there is a free car park in the trees on the left. The walk is waymarked from here and runs along the crest of the east hill overlooking Encombe House. There may be sheep in the field though, so take care. More fine views of coast and countryside on this walk.

WALK 63   SWYRE HEAD, PURBECK
DURATION: *approximately 1 hour.*
STARTING POINT: *Kingston.*
FOOD: *Scott Arms, Kingston. Well behaved dogs and children welcome.*

From Corfe Castle drive up the hill to Kingston. Turn right by the Scott Arms (a stupendous view of Corfe from their pub garden) and drive to the end of the road where you will find a small, rough, free car park. The walk takes you across fields and alongside Polar Wood with fine views of the golden bowl of Encombe House, nestling in its valley which runs to the sea. On top of the headland (666 ft) at the end of the path is an earthen mound with a stone seat on its summit. It is said that, with binoculars, on a very clear day it is possible to see the Cherbourg peninsula in France from this spot. (Focus just to the right of the wooden seat.) I am never quite sure if I HAVE seen it, or if I have spotted a passing ship!

WALK 64   HILL BOTTOM, PURBECK
DURATION: *approximately 1 hour.*
STARTING POINT: *Worth Matravers.*
FOOD: *Scott Arms, Kingston. Well behaved dogs and children welcome.*

Drive through the pretty stone-built village of Worth Matravers, leaving the duck pond on your left and go to the end of the road. At Renscombe Farm (Renscombe = Valley of the ravens) you will see a signpost indicating the car park which is a few yards along the rough track to St Albans Head. Walk back to Renscombe Farm and follow the track downhill through a gate. Hill Bottom is a tiny pretty hamlet hidden away in a fold of the hills. At the bottom of the track there are yellow waymarkers which lead back over a small stream and eventually climb steeply back up the grassy path to the car park. There are beautiful views across the cliffs and sea to Portland on this walk and in summer the area abounds with wild flowers and butterflies.

WALK 65   THORNCOMBE WOOD/BLACK HEATH
DURATION: *flexible.*
STARTING POINT: *Car Park, Thomas Hardy's Cottage, Bockhampton.*
FOOD: *The Blue Vinney, Puddletown. Dogs welcome.*

From the A35, midway between Puddletown and Dorchester, take the Bockhampton road and after half a mile follow the signs to Thomas Hardy's Cottage, birthplace of the world famous Dorset author in 1840. From the free car park there are trails through the 46 acre wood and leading to the adjoining 20 acres of Black Heath. In the car park is an information board where descriptive leaflets can be bought and which request you to keep to defined paths. This is a wildlife sanctuary and if you are fortunate you may see the tracks of fox, roe deer, badger and squirrel.

WALK 66   SUTTON POYNTZ, WHITE HORSE HILL
DURATION: *flexible.*
STARTING POINT: *The Springhead car park, Sutton Poyntz.*
FOOD: *The Springhead. Dogs welcome in public bar.*

This delightful village with its stream and ducks is a good starting place for a walk to White Horse Hill (518 ft). Park at the Inn if you intend visiting it later (recommended) and turn right until the road changes to a track. Turn right again here and you will see the waymarked footpath. This walk is steep in places but affords fine views over the downland, valleys and coastline as far as Portland.

WALK 67   RINGSTEAD
DISTANCE: *approx $3\frac{1}{2}$ miles circular, but extendible.*
STARTING POINT: *National Trust car park, top of Ringstead Hill.*
FOOD: *The Springhead Inn, Sutton Poyntz, and in summer, Beach Cafe, Ringstead.*

From the A353 at Warmwell roundabout, take the Weymouth road and then turn sharp left just after Poxwell with its Elizabethan manor house. Instead of driving down to the bay, keep straight on to the National Trust car park on top of the hill (472 ft) with views across Weymouth bay to Portland. Walk along the crest of the hill to a gate where waymarked footpaths guide you on an interesting circular walk down to the bay and back to the car park across fields. It is usually possible for this walk to be 'off the lead' in its entirety, depending on the presence of livestock. It may be extended to include the headland to the east, White Nothe, with its eye catching coastguard cottages silhouetted on the skyline. Just off the path down to the bay there is a tiny wooden chapel with gravestones, right on the cliff's edge - what a tranquil burial ground! At low tide, a rocky reef is exposed parallel with the beach, forming an unusual lagoon. A snack bar/shop in the car park sells drinks, fruit, sandwiches and ice-cream for your refreshment before you climb back up the hill.

WALK 68   MAUMBURY RINGS
DURATION: *short walk.*
STARTING POINT: *Traffic lights south of Dorchester market.*
FOOD: *Cornwall Hotel, Alexander Road. Dogs welcome. See walk 69.*

On the opposite side of the Weymouth road from Dorchester Market, just by the traffic lights you will see a grassy area with earthworks. This is Maumbury Rings, and a good place to let your dog run free if you have been around the town or the Wednesday morning market (well worth a visit, but if it is busy may I suggest you take it in turns with your human companion, if you have one, and stay at the Rings with your dog. A busy market is no place for him!).

Originally constructed as a Neolithic henge, the Romans adapted it as an amphitheatre and then during the Civil War it was incorporated in the defences of Dorchester. Its chequered history records that in 1705 an unfortunate Mary Channing was executed by burning in the arena and until 1766 the county gallows stood on the western side - a far cry from the peaceful place it is today.

WALK 69   MAIDEN CASTLE
DURATION: *flexible.*
STARTING POINT: *Maiden Castle car park, outskirts of Dorchester.*
FOOD: *Cornwall Hotel, Alexander Road. This is the most dog-friendly pub I know. There were five doggy regulars there on my last visit, all known to the Landlord by name. He greets each arrival - even strange dogs - with a dog biscuit. A lovely friendly atmosphere with plenty of genuine old Dorset characters as well - and those puddings!!*

From the A354 Dorchester to Weymouth road, Maiden Castle is on your right just outside Dorchester. There is a free car park at the end of the lane but at times dogs must be on a lead when livestock is grazing. An ancient Iron Age hill fort, some 440 ft above sea level, its defences enclose around 47 acres and at the eastern end you can still see the site of a Roman temple. There are explanatory boards at strategic points giving information about the site. Fine views extend to the horizon from its windswept ramparts.

A great walk for you and your dog - provided there are no restrictions.

WALK 70   HARDY'S MONUMENT
DURATION: *flexible.*
STARTING POINT: *Car park, Martinstown/Abbotsbury narrow road.*
FOOD: *Brewers Arms, Martinstown. Dogs outside only.*

At 777 ft above sea level this 72 ft high monument is a land and sea mark for miles around. It commemorates Nelson's Hardy, not the Wessex author Thomas Hardy as might be expected, as the former was born at nearby Portesham in 1769. It is not a thing of beauty - in fact it has been likened to a factory chimney - but the views over the surrounding countryside to Chesil Beach, Weymouth and Portland compensate for this. There are many footpaths leading from the free car park by the monument for you to explore.